Images of America
Oregon Coast Highway

This scene along the Roosevelt/Oregon Coast Highway from 1923 shows the narrow lanes and rough surface typical of the early construction. (Oregon Department of Transportation.)

ON THE COVER: A driver leaves his automobile to contemplate a view of the ocean along a stretch of the highway south of the city of Waldport. (Oregon Department of Transportation.)

IMAGES of America
OREGON COAST HIGHWAY

Laura E. Wilt

ARCADIA
PUBLISHING

Copyright © 2018 by Laura E. Wilt
ISBN 978-1-4671-0337-4

Published by Arcadia Publishing
Charleston, South Carolina

Printed in the United States of America

Library of Congress Control Number: 2018964384

For all general information, please contact Arcadia Publishing:
Telephone 843-853-2070
Fax 843-853-0044
E-mail sales@arcadiapublishing.com
For customer service and orders:
Toll-Free 1-888-313-2665

Visit us on the Internet at www.arcadiapublishing.com

To my husband, Michael, for his unfailing support, encouragement, and love.

Contents

Acknowledgments		6
Introduction		7
1.	The Beginnings	9
2.	Construction on the Northern Coast	15
3.	Construction on the Central Coast	31
4.	Construction on the Southern Coast	45
5.	Jeweled Clasps along a Matched String of Pearls	61
6.	Pushing toward the Sea	73
7.	Oregon State Parks and the Highway Department	91
8.	Lighthouses of the Oregon Coast	103
9.	Impact of the Oregon Coast Highway	109
10.	The Final Chapter	119
Bibliography		127

ACKNOWLEDGMENTS

There have been many who have contributed to the creation of this book, from words of encouragement to active help in gathering information. While it would be impossible to list them all, there are some who I would like to mention. First of all, thank you to friends and family who gave me the push I needed to take on this project. Special thanks to Patricia Solomon, for agreeing to provide edits, as well as my daughters and daughter-in-law, who also graciously added their comments and suggestions.

My thanks to the residents of the Oregon coast I met while working on the book for their sincere interest in having the story told. Among these, I would like to recognize the volunteers and members of the many local historical societies along the Oregon coast, whose commitment to their communities and passion for their history and local stories have served to preserve the past that is woven into the fiber of the present. Their work made this project easier. In particular, I would like to acknowledge Laurel Gerkman from the Curry County Historical Society, Jim Proehl from the Bandon Historical Society, Krissy Sonniksen from the Lincoln County Historical Society, and Debra Semrau and Steve Greif from the Coos County Historical Society. I would also like to thank Steve Saubert of Sea Lions Cave for sharing not only photographs and information, but also his enthusiasm for this natural wonder. Finally, thank you to Christy Sweet of the Oregon Parks and Recreation Department for sharing her expertise and opening her collection to me, and to Robert Melbo of the Oregon Department of Transportation Rail Division for his insight on the history of rail development along the coast. Any and all mistakes made in the telling of the story of the Oregon Coast Highway are entirely my own.

Many of the place names along the Oregon coast are pronounced differently than they might appear. A few of these include:

Coquille	ko-KEEL
Heceta	he-SEE-ta
Neahkanie	NEE-uh-kah-nee
Necanicum	neh-KAN-i-kum
Nehalem	neh-HAY-lum
Neskowin	NESS-ko-win
Netarts	NEE-tarts
Siuslaw	sye-YOO-slaw
Yachats	YAH-hahts
Yaquina	yə-KWIN-ə

Abbreviations used in courtesy lines include:

Bandon HS	Bandon Historical Society
BPR	Bureau of Public Roads, precursor of the FHWA
Coos Co. HS	Coos County Historical Society
Lincoln Co. HS	Lincoln County Historical Society
Nehalem Valley HS	Nehalem Valley Historical Society
ODOT	Oregon Department of Transportation
OSHD	Oregon State Highway Department
Parks	Oregon Parks and Recreation Department

INTRODUCTION

In 1913, bowing to pressure from the Good Roads movement and the increasing number of automobiles being registered in Oregon, the state legislature created the Oregon State Highway Commission, with the directive to "get Oregon out of the mud." The commission, which consisted of Gov. Oswald West, Secretary of State Ben Olcott, and state treasurer Thomas McKay, hired Maj. Henry Bowlby, a West Point graduate and engineer, to act as state highway engineer. The commission tasked Bowlby with compiling and presenting a system of highways that would provide year-round access for people traveling within the state.

From the mid-1800s, enterprising pioneers had blazed trails and wagon roads connecting the settlers coming to the Oregon country to their ultimate destinations—often in the fertile Willamette Valley. Eventually, county and territorial roadways were established. For Bowlby, these existing travel routes, however primitive, served as the backbone for his proposed system of state highways. However, the townships springing up along the Pacific Coast were, for the most part, far removed from the rest of the state. Cut off from the valley by the Coast Range mountains and separated from one another by the rugged headlands that characterized the coastline, these communities were tied most closely to the ocean and the rivers that emptied into it. Bowlby conceived of a highway that would stretch along the coastline from Washington to California, but when he presented his proposed highway system in 1914, the coastal highway was still largely a vision.

Creating a continuous all-season highway would take 12 years and over $28 million to complete—approximately $75,000 per mile for the total 384-mile stretch. The road was, in many places, hewn out of virgin forests and across rugged headlands using steam-powered equipment that today would seem very primitive. In some cases, materials and equipment had to be brought to locations by boat. Compounding these obstacles were the often unpredictable weather conditions; in areas that received more than 80 inches of rainfall per year, along with severe winter storms, operations often had to be reduced or halted during the winter months.

The highway was constructed in sections, and the order of construction was dependent on many variables, including travel needs, the procurement of right-of-way, and approval by the Bureau of Public Roads, as well as planning and consultation with the respective counties. Curry County officials, for example, requested that the most impassable sections be given precedence. For this reason, the heaviest grading work was done first, making the early construction costs greater than later expenditures for less difficult work.

Bridges would play an important role in the highway's story. Whether crossing small streams or spanning the wide coastal bays and rivers, bridges provided the links needed for uninterrupted travel along the ocean shores. With master bridge builder Conde McCullough at the helm of the highway department's bridge department, many of the bridges exhibited his signature Art Nouveau and Gothic architectural features.

The highway opened access to many previously isolated areas of the coast, creating economic and recreational opportunities that were widely welcomed and anticipated. There were, however, downsides for some residents. Buildings and businesses were moved or destroyed, and properties were sometimes divided to create the right-of-way necessary for construction. The Bandon *Western World* newspaper reported in a front-page story on January 24, 1923, that landowners were being offered $200 per acre by the highway commission for right-of-way, but there were a number of hold-outs.

Ultimately, despite all obstacles, the Oregon Coast Highway was officially completed in 1936 with the opening of the five major coastal bridges that were designed and constructed within the two-year span of 1934–1936. Subsequent improvements and realignments would continue to take place over time to optimize the safety and scenic beauty for the traveling public. It would take until the mid-1960s, however, before the final link was put in place for a continuous coastal highway spanning from Canada to the border with Mexico. The Astoria-Megler Bridge, crossing the Columbia River, was completed in 1966. This bridge replaced the last of the state-run ferry systems and provided a connection between Oregon and Washington.

The highway has undergone several name changes throughout the years, including Roosevelt Coast Military Highway, Roosevelt Coast Highway, and Oregon Coast Highway, often shortened to simply the "Coast Highway." It is also known by its US route number, 101. To avoid confusion, the name Coast Highway or Oregon Coast Highway is used throughout this book except in cases where specific references are made to other names. The photographs used in this book span the decades from the early 20th century to the mid-1960s, although the emphasis is on the early days of the highway's construction. Unless otherwise noted, cited reports and correspondence from the Oregon State Highway Department are unpublished documents located in the files of the Oregon Department of Transportation History Center.

This book does not claim to tell the complete record of the highway or of the cities and towns through which it passes; each community, wayside, overlook, and cove has its own story and history. The purpose of this narrative is simply to provide a glimpse into the process and impact of the highway's construction.

One
THE BEGINNINGS

In 1913, Oregon governor Oswald West, chair of the newly formed Oregon State Highway Commission, appealed to the state legislature to declare the beaches from Astoria to the California border to be part of the state highway system. While this did not establish an alignment for the coastal highway, it was the first step in making it a reality. (ODOT.)

The idea of utilizing the beaches as highways was not a new one. Portions of the beaches had long been used to transport freight and passengers, and at least one county—Coos—had designated the beaches within its borders as a county highway. This type of travel could be treacherous, with coaches having to wait for low tide to make the dash around headlands. (Coos Co. HS.)

Some of the beach routes had even been carved out of the headlands, such as this example of Hug Point near Cannon Beach. Automobiles began to replace horse-drawn stages; Vern Gorst and Charles King developed an auto stage line that ran between North Bend and Marshfield (now Coos Bay) in 1912, and the Coos Bay–Florence Fast Freight Company purchased a fleet of Fords in 1914 to offer faster travel along the beach route. (Lincoln Co. HS.)

However, travel by automobile along the beaches sometimes proved to be problematic. Saltwater splashed into the engines, and the heavy cars often became stuck in the soft sand. In a 1991 article in the *Oregon Coast* magazine, Gary Meier wrote of a time when one of the auto stages got stuck fording the mouth of Ten Mile Creek: "It had to be dismantled and taken piece by piece across the creek, where it was reassembled and sent chugging on its way," the article related. Incoming tides also caught unwary drivers by surprise. Despite the sand proving to be a formidable environment for automobiles, the establishment of the beaches as part of the state highway system laid the groundwork for the growth of the state park system as well as providing public access to all beaches in the state. (Lincoln Co. HS.)

In addition to beach travel, other areas of the coastline were served by primitive wagon roads, such as this one at Cape Perpetua. In many cases, though, the coastal communities were completely cut off from one another except for foot trails. By the time the highway commission was formed, only a handful of stretches had improved roads that could easily accommodate automobiles. (Lincoln Co. HS.)

11

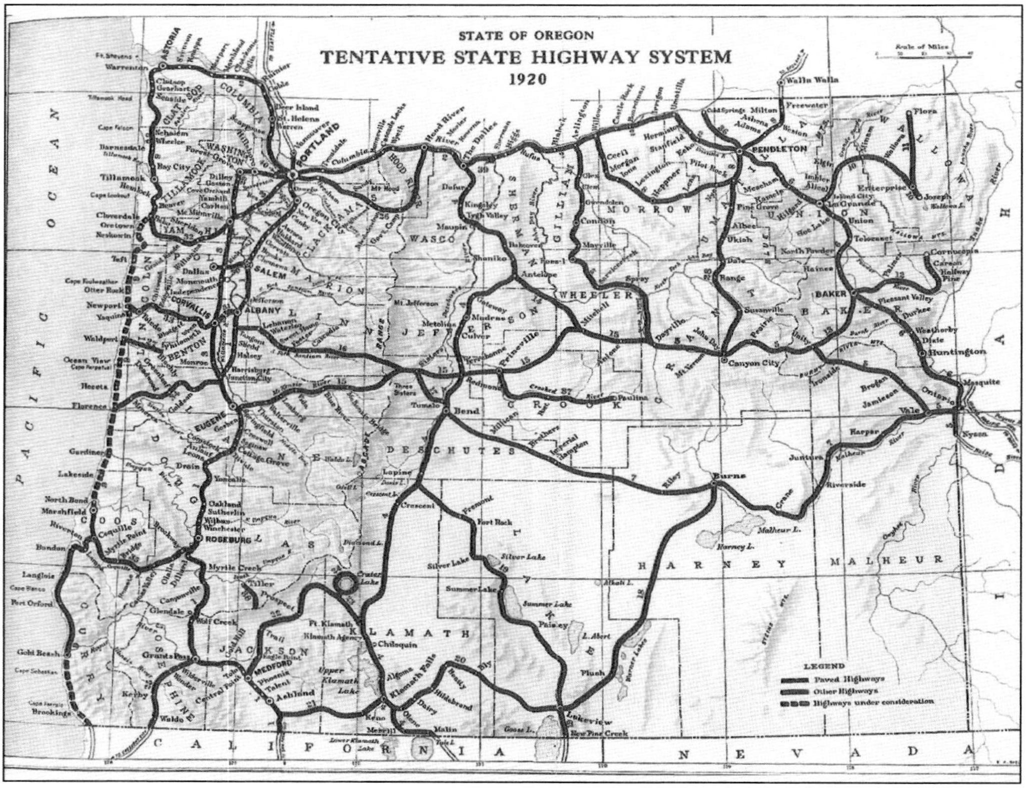

In 1917, with the reorganization of the State Highway Commission into a functioning highway department, the state highway system proposed by Maj. Henry Bowlby, the first state highway engineer, was formally adopted. Most of the system was aligned along existing county and territorial highways, but as seen by the dotted lines in this map from the *1919–1920 Biennial Report of the Highway Commission*, the majority of the Oregon Coast Highway was only a proposed route. Several areas that had seen early development were designated as the Coast Highway. (ODOT.)

Also in 1917, the state made a lengthy and impassioned appeal to the federal government to establish a military highway along the length of the Oregon coast. The argument cited earlier military highways that had also been used by the public, as well as the need for the ability to move troops in the event of an invasion. The report stated, "Any roads built by Federal aid would essentially be commercial highways for the development of the State, but would be so located as to be of great value for military purposes." It went on to state the military need: "With the enormous increase of wealth and importance of the Pacific Coast, the danger of attack and invasion can no longer be ignored. Especially is this true because of the smallness of the navy, the length of our sea coast and our lack of communication with the coast." (ODOT.)

In 1919, Lincoln County resident and legislator Ben Jones presented a bill authorizing the construction of the highway along the coast. Jones is credited with the name Roosevelt Coast Military Highway, named after one of his favorite presidents, Theodore Roosevelt. The measure was sent to the voters and passed in June 1919 with a 2-1 margin. A full-page ad in Bandon's *Western World* newspaper from May 29, 1919, encouraged voters to support the bill. The 1919 legislation called for the state to appropriate $2.5 million, half of the estimated $5 million cost to build the highway—to be turned over to the federal government for the construction of a military highway that would be owned and maintained by the United States. (Lincoln Co. HS.)

Despite the lack of commitment on the part of the US government, construction commenced on the coast highway. However, by 1921, it became clear that the federal military highway designation would not materialize. The state and the coastal counties were determined that work on the highway would continue, so rather than pursuing a federal classification, new state legislation placed the Roosevelt Coast Highway on the Oregon state highway system. The highway was eligible for federal-aid highway funding, however, and a considerable amount of federal dollars went into its construction. By 1931, the Oregon legislature decided to drop the name that had been attached to the concept of a federal military highway and renamed the Roosevelt Coast Highway the simpler Oregon Coast Highway, OSHD Highway No. 9. The city of Bandon announced the highway with this welcome arch for visitors. Later, the name Roosevelt Highway would be replaced by Oregon Coast Highway on the signs. (Bandon HS.)

Grading and surfacing produced an all-season roadway. The most common hard surface finish was bituminous macadam, which consisted of crushed stone with a binder of tar and/or asphalt. (ODOT.)

In 1926, the American Association of State Highway Officials (AASHO) had developed and approved a system of routes that would link highways across state lines. The Oregon Coast Highway was included in this initial designation, linking the highway in Oregon with coastal highways in California and Washington, together forming US Route 101. While US and state route numbers were eventually assigned to all of the highways in the state highway system, the highway department continued to use the unique highway number—in this case, OSHD Highway No. 9—or the highway name for internal departmental use. (ODOT.)

Two

Construction on the Northern Coast

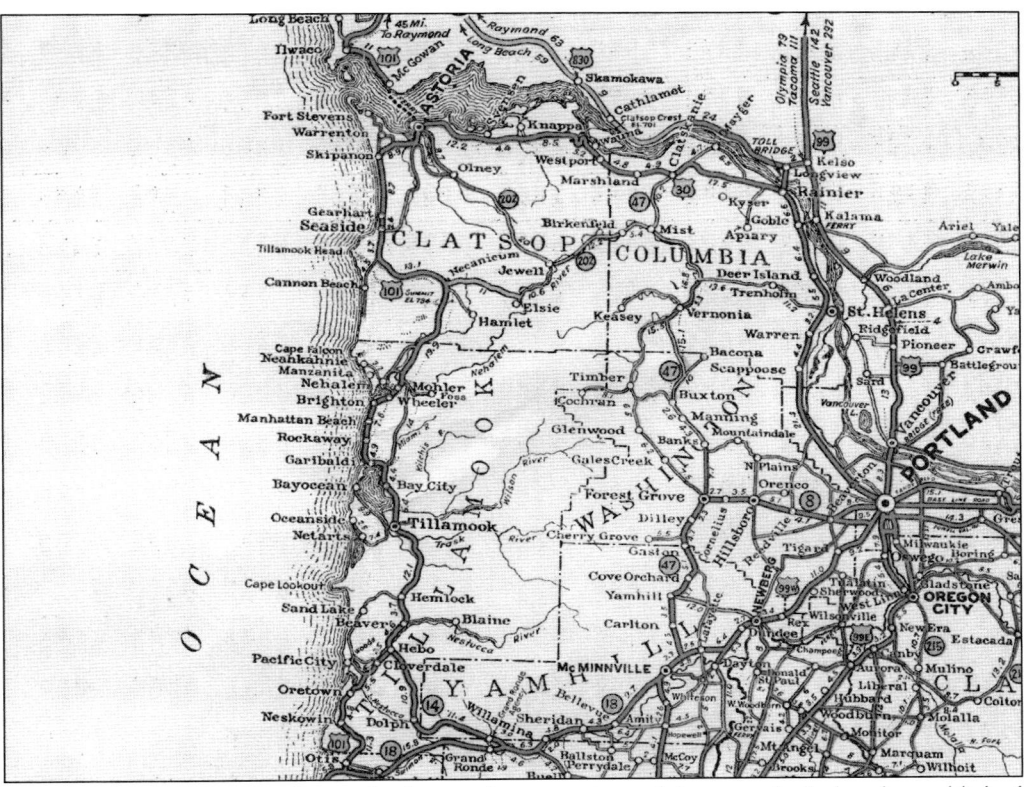

Unlike their neighbors to the south, the northern portions of the coast had already established a system of county roads prior to the planning of the Coast Highway. Due in part to their proximity to the Columbia River, the area had been settled and developed fairly early. With the influx of wealthy Portlanders escaping the summer heat in the Willamette Valley on steamboats along the Columbia, the area from Astoria to the Tillamook County line saw improved—even paved—roadways before the state took over the task of establishing a year-round route from the Columbia River boundary with Washington to the California border. This is a detail from the 1936 state highway map. (ODOT.)

First settled as a fur-trading post, the city of Astoria at the mouth of the Columbia River lays claim to being the oldest settlement west of the Rockies. By the late 1800s, the town enjoyed thriving fishing, cannery, wood products, and shipping industries. By the turn of the 20th century, Astoria was linked to Portland via a rail line that not only transported freight, but also became a popular passenger line. This photograph shows the Astoria docks as seen from the highway in 1920. (ODOT.)

Until the bridge across the Columbia River at Astoria was completed in 1966 to close the gap on US Route 101 between Oregon and Washington, a ferry served to carry passengers across the Columbia River. This was the loading area for the ferry in 1939. (ODOT.)

Clatsop County took on the improvement of county roads with the assistance of state funds in 1914 as part of the earlier Columbia River Highway. A 1916 report from the district engineer to state engineer John Lewis related that the stretch from Astoria to Warrenton was paved with an eight-foot concrete pavement with four-foot macadam shoulders on either side—a pavement method also used by the state on the Pacific Highway in the Sexton Mountain area in Josephine County. The paving was done late in the fall of 1914 under the direction of state highway engineer Henry Bowlby. The report states, "This work was done late in the season and was not very satisfactory locally as traffic was interfered with and practically stopped. For some time machinery did not work well and very little was accomplished, and this caused quite a lot of local complaint about waste of money, etc. The pavement was talked over the county far and wide as a failure." Despite this negative summary, on traveling over the route a year after construction, the district engineer felt that the roadway was in good shape except for a few areas where the concrete did not seem to have set properly, so it is unclear if the perceived failure was actually from the road itself or from the inconvenience it caused to the local residents. This 1914 photograph shows a road superintendent conducting an equipment inventory in the Astoria area. (ODOT.)

Part of the existing roadway south of Astoria was a plank road, consisting of wood planks laid across the road surface. The planking was taken up as the highway was constructed. (ODOT.)

There were tensions in Clatsop County between local road districts and the state regarding construction plans and highway alignment. With roads between Astoria and Gearhart in poor condition, the county decided to act before the state finalized construction plans. The 1916 district engineer's report stated that the county acted out of "fear that the state would step in and build on their own survey, and in hope that if they made a good, well improved road out of the old one before the State got ready, it would be adopted." While acknowledging that the county "definitely abandoned our survey," the state district engineer reported that the result was that this "produced very quick results at very little expense to the State." (ODOT.)

While Astoria's economy depended primarily on industry and shipping for its wealth, its neighbors to the south were already well-established as vacation destinations for travelers to the coast before the Coast Highway was constructed. Seaside is said to have been named for the luxurious mansion built in the 1870s by railroad tycoon Ben Holladay. He named the residence Seaside House and entertained prominent friends, leading to the popularity of the area for wealthy travelers. A rail line between Astoria and Seaside was established in 1890, allowing passengers to transfer from steamers sailing down the Columbia River to catch the train at Young's Bay in Astoria for the short trip to Seaside. By the time the rail line from Portland to Astoria was completed a decade later, Seaside was a destination for families to escape the heat of Portland and the Willamette Valley for the summer months. The passenger line gained the nickname of the "Daddy Train," allowing fathers to leave their offices in Portland to spend the weekend on the coast with their families, returning to work on Monday morning. (ODOT.)

Seaside's broad, sloping beaches are a result in part of the jetties built at the mouth of the Columbia River, completed around 1917. Paving and improvement projects north of the city and within the city limits in 1914 and 1915, combined with the construction of the Promenade and the deepening of the beaches from the jetty construction, served to greatly increase the city's attraction to tourists. The beaches and the iconic Seaside Promenade, with its distinctive turnaround, can clearly be seen in the postcard on the previous page and in this 1961 aerial view. The Promenade had originally been a wooden boardwalk, but the concrete version still popular today was constructed in the 1920s. (ODOT.)

In the designation of the earlier east-west Columbia River Highway, Seaside marked the southwestern-most point, being considered the "end of the Oregon Trail," or the "end of the Lewis and Clark Trail." When the Roosevelt Coast Military Highway was designated by the Oregon legislature in 1919, it defined the highway as running from the city of Astoria to the California state line. The western point of the Columbia River Highway was pushed back to the junction with the Coast Highway. This photograph shows the intersection of Route 101 and Roosevelt Drive at the northern limits of Seaside. (ODOT.)

The 1914 report by Major Bowlby to the State Highway Commission reported that an area near Seaside had been paved with Warrenite paving. The report describes the process: "After the sub-grade was prepared to conform to the standard cross-section, forms were set to hold the 'hot stuff,' or Warrenite surface." This photograph shows a crew laying down the "hot stuff." (ODOT.)

While the county road was surfaced for the first few miles south of Seaside, the route quickly deteriorated into a footpath from there to the Tillamook County line. Clatsop County, with direction from the state, worked to improve this section during the period of 1915–1916. By the time the 1919–1920 biennial report was published, the entire stretch between Seaside and the Tillamook County line, with the exception of a one-and-a-half-mile stretch under contract, had been macadamized. (ODOT.)

The original alignment of the highway stretched inland south of Tillamook Head, heading toward the town of Necanicum. A county road provided access from the Coast Highway to the resort town of Cannon Beach, but the highway itself bypassed the town for several years. This photograph shows Haystack Rock off Cannon Beach. (ODOT.)

The town was named for this cannon that washed up nearby from the wreckage of the USS *Shark* in 1846. Originally called Elk Creek, the name was officially changed in 1922. The cannon was displayed in front of an early lodging establishment in the area. The broad beaches and beautiful scenery made Cannon Beach a popular vacation destination, and pressure was put on the state to realign the Coast Highway to include the town. (ODOT.)

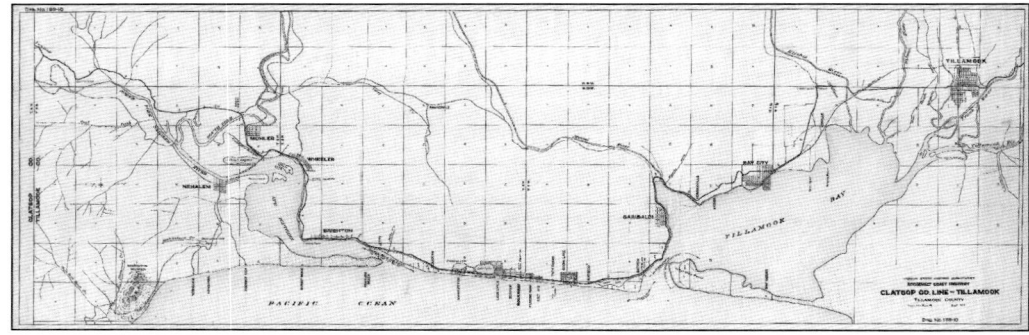

Work on the highway from the Clatsop County line south into Tillamook County began in the early 1920s, with much of the grading work done by the county; once grading was completed, the state followed up with the work of surfacing. (ODOT.)

Wheeler, located on Nehalem Bay, was established in the early 1900s as a mill town, as was the township of Brighton to the south of Wheeler. The Coast Highway is in the foreground in this photograph of Wheeler. (ODOT.).

Portions of the original roadway included planked sections, and the portion between Jetty Creek, south of Wheeler, and Brighton was undeveloped. By 1927, the highway had been largely completed south to the city of Tillamook. Here, work is being done on the Jetty Creek to Brighton section. (ODOT.)

This 1922 photograph shows clearing of right-of-way for the highway in Tillamook County. Clearing and grading was often handled under one contract, with the surfacing done later under a separate contract. (ODOT.)

Sandwiched between the mill towns of Wheeler and Brighton to the north and Garibaldi to the south, Rockaway Beach was a well-known resort before the highway was constructed through there in the 1920s. Originally accessible only via the wide beaches that extended from Garibaldi to Nehalem Bay prior to the construction of jetties, passenger rail service came to Rockaway Beach in 1912. Much like Seaside—although on a smaller scale—the area became a popular summer vacation spot, with fathers arriving by train for a weekend visit with their families. The construction of the Coast Highway opened up tourist travel to automobiles. This aerial photograph from 1929 shows the highway running through the length of the town. (Parks.)

The distinctive rock formations off the coast gave the small community of Twin Rocks its name. South of Rockaway Beach, this town was formed as a summer resort destination, with the post office established in 1914. (ODOT.)

This photograph shows the highway through the town of Garibaldi, named by an early landowner in honor of the Italian statesman Giuseppe Garibaldi. Located on Tillamook Bay, the town was well known for its fishing industry and wood mills. (ODOT.)

The highway followed the east side of Tillamook Bay for several miles before returning to the coast. (ODOT.)

Here, sea stacks—columns of rock formed over time by wind and water—are seen along the coast of Tillamook Bay. (ODOT.)

The mild, damp coastal weather yields lush grass that supported the dairy industry in Tillamook County, as well as other areas of the coast. Fields of dairy cows remain a common site for travelers along the Coast Highway in Tillamook County. (ODOT.)

This bridge north of the city of Tillamook is being demolished as part of an improvement project on the highway. Curious onlookers have gathered to watch the progress. (ODOT.)

For many people, the name *Tillamook* is synonymous with cheese and ice cream. The first cheese factory was built in 1893, and in 1909, several regional cheesemakers formed the Tillamook County Creamery Association. Product was originally shipped to markets in Astoria and Portland by boat, but the opening of the highway created a more direct means of transporting cheese and other dairy products. In 1949, the four largest independent cheese plants in the Tillamook area merged and built a large cheese-making plant along the Coast Highway in Tillamook. The Tillamook Cheese Factory quickly became a point of interest for the traveling public. (Oregon Historical Society.)

The Tillamook Cheese Factory grew over the years, and its proximity to the Coast Highway continued to draw visitors to sample the cheese and ice cream produced at the facility. (ODOT.)

A bit south of the city of Tillamook, a five-mile stretch of the highway was improved in 1917 for military purposes during World War I. This portion supported heavy traffic from trucks hauling spruce timber for the war effort, causing the surface to break down. The section was resurfaced in 1921. (ODOT.)

The original alignment of the Coast Highway south of Tillamook turned inland and included the town of Hebo. Later projects would push the highway closer to the coast in this area, but Hebo remained the junction with the McMinnville-Tillamook Highway, the important connection with the Willamette Valley that was completed in 1922. This glass-slide photograph shows that highway near Hebo. (ODOT.)

29

The work south of Hebo to Neskowin was completed with a combination of county and state forces between 1922 and 1923. Here, a crew is using a Caterpillar to haul snags. (ODOT.)

Three

CONSTRUCTION ON THE CENTRAL COAST

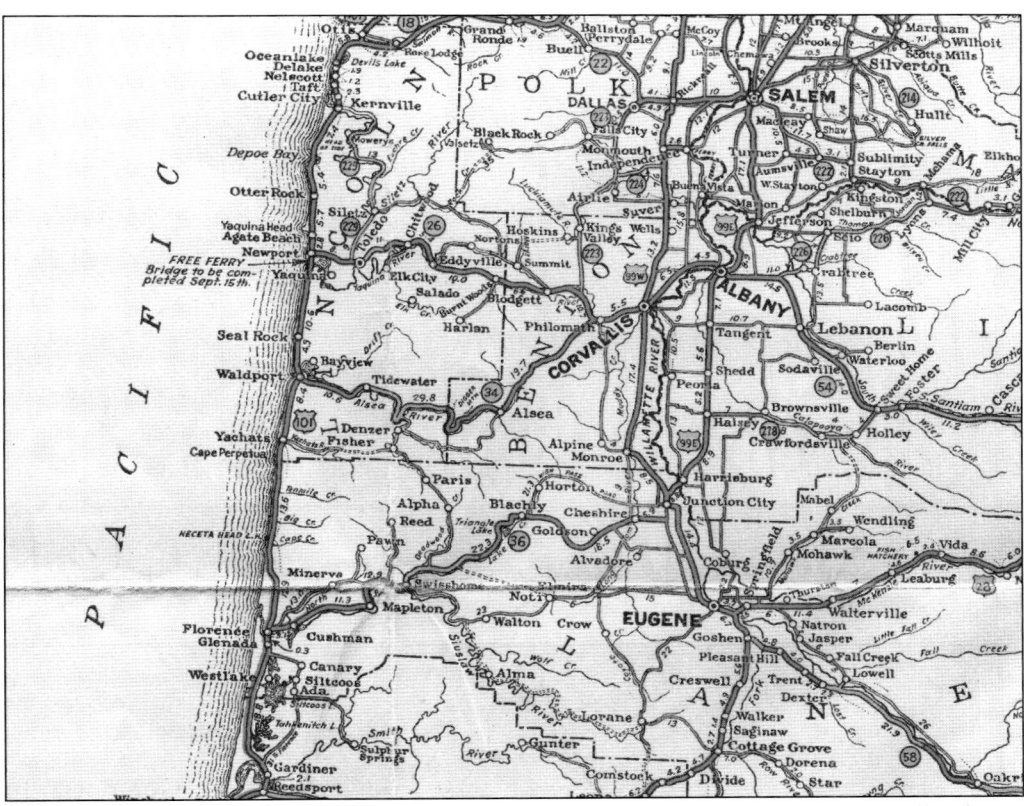

The central Oregon coast is generally considered to include the area from the headland area known as Cascade Head south to the city of Reedsport. This is a detail from the 1936 state highway map. (ODOT.)

Just south of Cascade Head lies modern-day Lincoln City. Prior to its incorporation in 1965, the area was divided into a number of adjacent communities including Oceanlake, DeLake, Nelscott, Taft, and Cutler City. This photograph shows the highway running through Oceanlake in 1949. (ODOT.)

The 1923 report on current conditions reported that "From Devil's Lake [north of Oceanlake] to Taft, 5.47 miles, the road is crooked and narrow and impassable in winter or after heavy storms." By the time that report had been written, the Bureau of Public Roads (BPR) had extended its Forest Road project that ran from Neskowin to Devils Lake to include the communities down to the Siletz River (see page 37). BPR awarded the contract for this portion in 1924. This photograph of holiday crowds in Taft shows the improved roadway attracting heavy traffic. (Lincoln Co. HS.)

South of Taft, the local road could "only be traveled in summer" and was "not much more than passable then." This portion of the coastline was very rugged and heavily timbered; the 1925–1926 biennial report stated that access was difficult and getting supplies and materials in place proved challenging, with "some of them coming by rail and then being hauled overland with horse teams, and others coming by boat." (ODOT.)

Boiler Bay was named for the boiler from the *J. Marhoffer* steam schooner, which wrecked in the area in 1910. The boiler made its way into the bay and can still be seen during very low tides. (Lincoln Co. HS.)

33

Depoe Bay was a town deeply rooted in the ocean and the fishing industry and lays claim to having the world's smallest navigable harbor. The town remains a popular spot for whale watching, particularly during the gray whale migration period. Here, townspeople and tourists line the highway bridge as boats leave for the yearly celebration to honor those lost at sea. (ODOT.)

Downtown Depoe Bay was well known for the spouting horns that shot spray high into the air, at times misting cars on the highway. (ODOT.)

South of Depoe Bay, nearing Otter Rock, this photograph gives an indication of the difficulty of laying the roadway along this section. Construction crews carved the highway from the cliffside in the headland area. (Parks.)

Near Otter Rock and Otter Crest State Park lies the bluff of Cape Foulweather, named by Capt. James Cook in the 1770s for the bad weather he and his crew encountered in the area. One of the attractions here was the Look-Out gift shop, originally opened as a coffee shop in 1937 by Wilber "Buck" Badley and his wife, Ann. The gift shop remained popular even after a later realignment left it off the direct route of the highway. The shop and overview are now under the control of the Oregon Parks and Recreation Department. With its spectacular panoramic views, the building was used as a military lookout post during World War II. (Parks.)

No road existed between Otter Rock and Agate Beach, north of the city of Newport, before the construction of the Coast Highway; the beach provided the only direct route, and this was dangerous and often impassable. This photograph was taken four miles north of Newport shortly after construction. (ODOT.)

Despite the contract for this stretch being awarded in early 1923, it would take over two years for the grading to be finished because the heavy clearing, grubbing, and grading work, combined with the lack of accessibility for supplies and materials, greatly slowed progress. By late 1925, the entire stretch between Otter Rock and Newport had been graded and surfaced with an all-season rock surface, as shown in this photograph just north of Newport. (ODOT.)

Newport was well known as a commercial fishing hub, but the city had established a solid reputation as a favorite destination for tourists and ocean visitors prior to the highway's construction. The Oregon Pacific Railroad provided access from the Willamette Valley to Yaquina City, and a short steamer ride connected passengers to the resorts of the city. Steamers also provided transportation to and from San Francisco. This photograph of the downtown area in 1950 shows a bustling city well accustomed to catering to visitors. Newport is located on Yaquina Bay, and a ferry provided service across the bay until the Yaquina Bay Bridge was completed in 1936. (Lincoln Co. HS.)

Below Newport, the highway skirted and then entered Siuslaw National Forest. When a state highway traveled through a national forest, it was considered a forest highway, and BPR took over much of the decision-making for projects, and often the construction itself. In the case of Forest Highway No. 5, which extended from Berry Creek to China Creek, the project included a number of contracts, some of which were handled by the state and others by BPR. This photograph shows a crew working near South Beach. (Lincoln Co. HS.)

When the United States entered World War I in 1917, the military had an immediate need for ships and airplanes. Sitka spruce was the material of choice for airplanes at the time, and the Army recognized that some of the best stands of these trees could be found in the Northwest. The Spruce Production Division was formed to harvest spruce and build rail lines to transport the timber to mills. But when the armistice was signed on November 11, 1918, production came to an abrupt halt. (Oregon State University Archives Collection.)

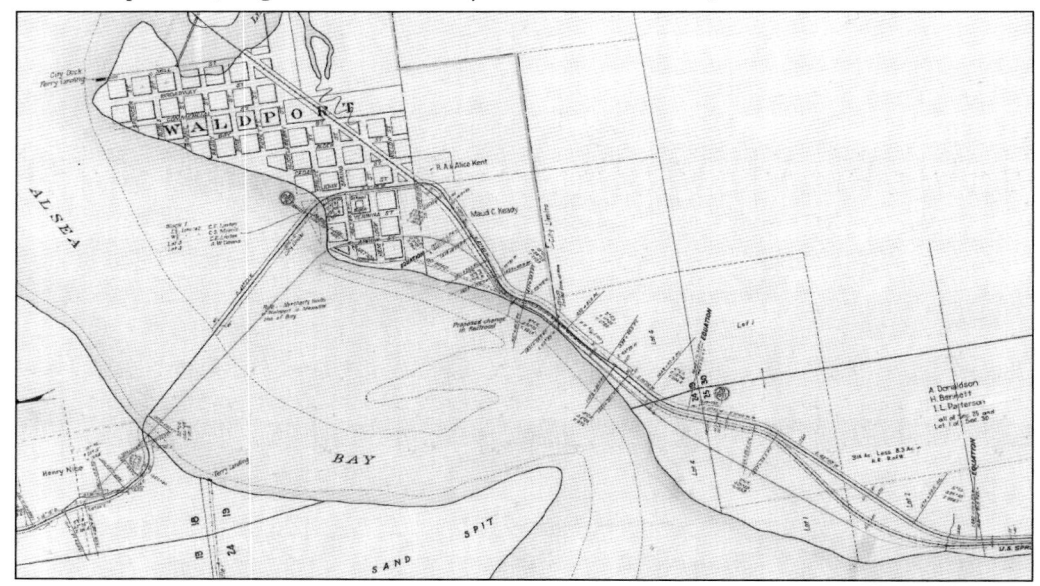

One of the areas purchased by the Army for timber was south of Waldport. By the time the war had ended, the crew working here had built the rail line—known as the Alsea Southern Railroad—across Alsea Bay and through the town of Waldport. While the Spruce Production lines were sold, many of the former rail beds were used for the construction of the highway. This map shows that the highway through Waldport took advantage of the existing rail right-of-way. (ODOT.)

The city of Waldport is situated at the tip of Alsea Bay. A ferry used to transport travelers across the bay until a bridge was completed in 1936. Along the stretch of highway south of town shown here, a seawall divided the road from the ocean. (ODOT.)

In the early part of the 20th century, the beach served as the only road from Waldport south to Yachats. The construction of the highway encouraged a rise in tourism to the area. This scene of the highway going through the town shows an example of tourist cabins available for visitors. (ODOT.)

Yachats served as the gateway to the rugged and spectacular Cape Perpetua, as seen here, showing the view from the summit. Like Cape Foulweather, this cape was named by Capt. James Cook on his voyage along the coast in the late 1770s. (ODOT.)

BPR was responsible for much of the roadway construction through the forest land, with its signature rock walls along the roadside, as seen in this image of the Heceta Head Lighthouse in the distance. (ODOT.)

The state, however, took on the design and construction of the Conde McCullough–designed bridge at Arch Cape, and the tunnel at its far end, seen here looking south from the lighthouse complex. (Parks.)

This photograph shows the tunnel more clearly during the construction phase of both bridge and tunnel. This area was opened to traffic in 1932. (ODOT.)

Just south of Heceta Head Lighthouse lies an enormous cavern billed as "America's largest sea cave." This cavern, which actually forms the main area of a series of caves, along with the rocky ledges outside the entrance, serves as an ideal breeding ground and winter shelter for hundreds of Steller sea lions. (ODOT.)

The land including the caves was purchased from the state in 1887 by a sea captain, William Cox. In 1927, local developer R.A. Clanton saw an opportunity to open the caves to the public and acquired the land from the Cox family. The circle at left indicates the south entrance to the main cave. (ODOT.)

When plans for the highway became certain, Clanton was joined with partners, and Sea Lion Caves was opened to the public in August 1932. Original access to the caves included a 1,500-foot-long pathway carved by hand out of the native basalt, with a 135-step wooden tower that led to the north entrance and the viewing area. The construction of an elevator, completed in 1961, resulted in a sharp increase in attendance by offering easy access to the caves. Sea Lion Caves remains a unique and extremely popular attraction along the coast. (Sea Lion Caves.)

This early postcard advertising the Sea Lion Caves shows the main cave area. The population of sea lions in the caves would swell to the hundreds in the winter. (ODOT.)

This aerial photograph of the city of Florence shows the iconic McCullough bridge across the Siuslaw River. The highway from Sutton Lake to Florence was graded during 1925–1926. This section proved to be challenging, since the terrain featured sand dunes with sparse timber and underbrush. Because of the tendency for substantial wind drift of the sand, a four-inch coat of clay was spread on the entire width of the surface. The grading work south of Florence into Douglas County was done in sections from 1928 to 1932. (ODOT.)

Four

Construction on the Southern Coast

The construction of the highway along the southern coast stretched from Reedsport in Douglas County to the California border. An early survey of the coastal conditions in Douglas County prior to the highway coming through determined simply, "No road along the coast, it is necessary to detour from Newport or Waldport to the Pacific Highway and back to the Coast from Roseburg to Marshfield [now Coos Bay]." This is a detail from the 1936 state highway map. (ODOT.)

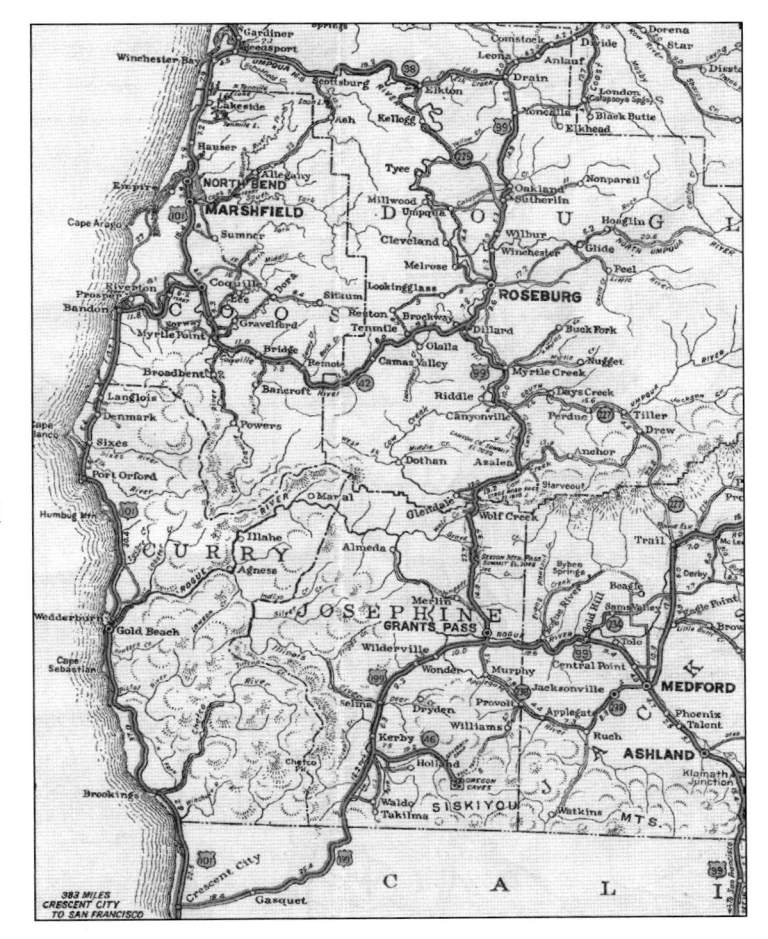

45

The highway in the Reedsport area of Douglas County was put under contract in 1926, and this August 1940 photograph shows a well-surfaced and well-traveled highway in Reedsport looking west from the east entrance into town. Reedsport was settled in a marshy area in the estuary of the Umpqua River, the second largest river between the Sacramento in California and the Columbia, forming the border between Oregon and Washington. It was an easily navigated river, and the early local economy depended on salmon fishing and processing. Eventually, logging took over as the primary industry in this area. A bridge replaced ferry service in 1936. (ODOT.)

South of the town of Winchester Bay, the highway curved around Clear Lake. A natural body of water among the coastal dunes, this lake serves even today as the water supply for Reedsport. The highway in Douglas County was put under contract in 1926 from Gardiner in the north through Lakeside in Coos County. (ODOT.)

According to Nathan Douthit in his book *The Coos Bay Region 1890–1944: Life on a Coastal Frontier*, there were only six miles of permanent roads in Coos County by 1911, lying between Empire City and Bastendorff Beach, the oceanfront estate of Louis J. Simpson, Shore Acres. By the time of Nunn's report, other improvements had been made, including a paved road from North Bend through Marshfield (now Coos Bay) to Coquille to accommodate traffic to the North Bend Ferry. The road from Bandon to the Curry County line was also paved with macadam. (Oregon State Archives.)

Although this photograph shows a stretch hugging the coastline, the original alignment routed the highway inland from Marshfield to Coquille and from Coquille to Bandon. The Marshfield-to-Coquille section was completed in 1921, and the contract for the highway between Coquille and Bandon was awarded in 1924. (ODOT.)

This image shows a section of roadway along Isthmus Inlet between Coquille and Marshfield (now Coos Bay) that was surfaced with concrete. (ODOT.)

The highway paralleled the Coquille River in portions of Coos County. Here, Port Orford cedar is awaiting the freshet, or spring thaw, in the mountains, which would swell the river and take the lumber downriver for processing. (ODOT.)

The December 16, 1915, edition of the *Western World* emphasized the isolation of Bandon. It highlighted the "three ways of getting to Bandon:" "take the steamer Elizabeth from San Francisco, fare $10.00; take either the Alliance or Breakwater from Portland to Marshfield, then take a train to Coquille at 9 o'clock, connection with the Coquille River boat, landing you at noon the same day in Bandon, combined fare, not counting lodgings is approx. $12;" and "over stage from Roseburg, Oregon to Myrtle Point, from which place you take the river boat to Bandon as before, fare being $5 for stage and $1 boat. We recommend boat clear through, in the wintertime at least. It is quicker and pleasanter for those not afflicted with seasickness." This photograph shows the beach below Bandon. (ODOT.)

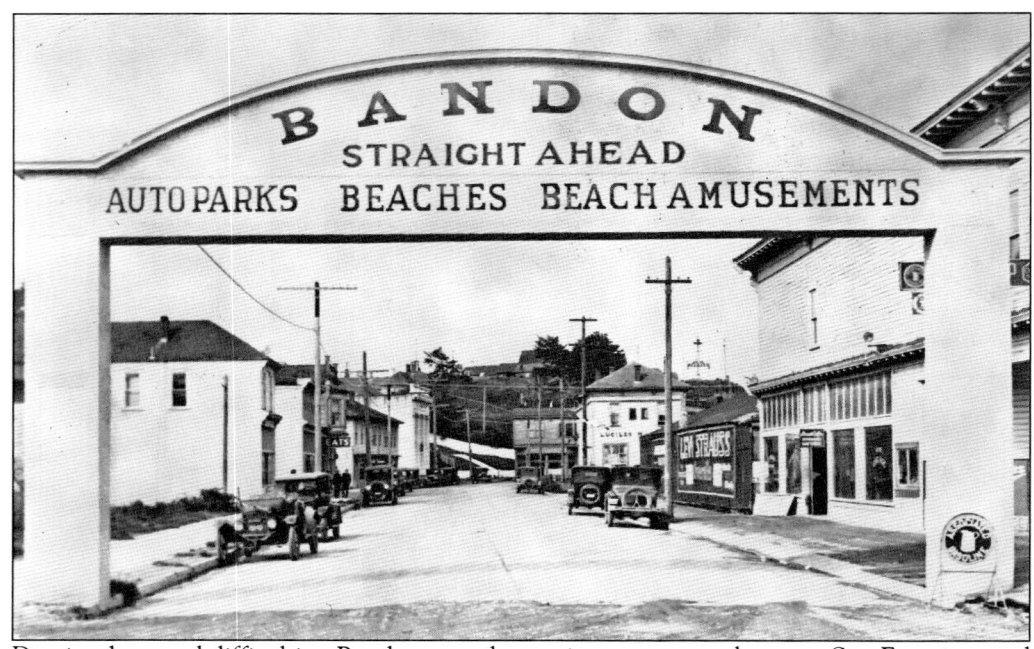

Despite the travel difficulties, Bandon served as an important port between San Francisco and Portland and had grown a reputation as a popular tourist location. Already billing itself as the most beautiful city on the southern Oregon coast, the city advertised its attractions on this archway built across the new highway. (Bandon HS.)

With the opening of the highway, the riverboats used to ferry passengers from Coquille to Bandon became obsolete, and the owner of the *Telegraph* and the *Dora* eventually ran the boats aground in a nearby field, abandoning them. (Bandon HS.)

Disaster struck Bandon on September 26, 1936, when shifting wind caused embers from a nearby wildfire to ignite buildings, and a blazing fire soon engulfed the business district. (ODOT.)

The final death toll stood at 13. The Bandon industrial district was virtually destroyed, and a large number of private homes burned in the conflagration. Many of the local residents escaped to the ocean beach to survive the intense fires, and local Coast Guard boats ferried survivors across the river to safety throughout the night. The city slowly rebuilt and eventually regained its reputation as a tourist destination. (ODOT.)

The coastal communities of Curry County were particularly isolated. No rail service was available at the time the highway was being planned, and shallow bars combined with unprotected coastline made travel by sea dangerous and unreliable. Early county roads were primitive and narrow, and most followed the trails blazed by the Native Americans. Arthur Dorn wrote for the *Curry County Reporter* that "the trail, later the road, which curled and twisted between Port Orford and California was awful. The road was unsurpassed anywhere in the world for hazards of rocks, tree roots, and bogs." Dorn elaborated, "Passengers riding the old horse-drawn stages were thrown forward and backward, up and down, first to one side, then to the other, until; they were sore, full of anguish and all but disjointed. With the appearance of automobiles the road was slightly improved by the venturesome few who worked their ways with picks and shovels." The rugged coastline can be seen in this photograph taken near Brookings. (ODOT.)

Contractor camps were common as the highway projects went in, as seen in this example in Curry County. Road construction on the highway made use of local manpower. The *Yaquina Bay News* reported on July 26, 1923, that "practically every man and boy over 14 years of age is employed on this road in some capacity, while most of the women on the farms are milking the cows and doing the chores." (Curry Co. HS.)

This photograph shows a 1930 auto caravan passing through the town of Langlois on its way from Marshfield (now Coos Bay) to Crescent City, California. (Brookings HS.)

The town of Port Orford was well known for the Port Orford cedar (also known as white cedar or Oregon cedar) lumber shipped from the port. The steamer *Frogner* is shown here loading a shipment of lumber. A root disease hit the area in the 1950s, destroying many of the native timber stands, but commercial fishing remained an important part of the local economy. (ODOT.)

The Roosevelt Highway is shown south of Port Orford, looking north to the town. This is an early example of grading and surfacing on the highway. While the road would later be improved, this provided a year-round surface for automobile travel. (Curry Co. HS.)

Another early Curry County photograph shows the highway following the coastline around the Humbug Mountain area. (Brookings HS.)

Frankport, just north of Ophir, was established as a port by the Frank Company tanners from San Francisco. The company harvested tanbark—tree bark used to produce tannins for the process of tanning animal hides—loading it onto schooners at the end of the point. This view shows the highway south of Frankport. (ODOT.)

Gold was discovered in the Rogue River in the 1850s. While large finds dwindled rather quickly, the promise of fortune led to the growth of the population along the length of the river. Later, the Rogue served as an important resource for the salmon industry. This photograph shows the highway following the river near the city of Wedderburn. (ODOT.)

Originally named Ellensburg, the settlement became known as Gold Beach with the discovery of gold at the mouth of the Rogue River in the early 1850s. While mining was largely replaced by the fishing industry by the following decade, the name stuck and became official in 1890. This undated photograph shows the highway running through the downtown area. (Curry Co. HS.)

56

A small ferry served automobiles crossing the Rogue River prior to the construction of the bridge. The limited capacity of the ferry proved inadequate for the increasing number of travelers, particularly in the summer months. (ODOT.)

When the McCullough-designed Rogue River Bridge between Gold Beach and Wedderburn opened to the public in 1932, the event was marked with a well-attended celebration. (Curry Co. HS.)

The highway traveled through forest areas south of Cape Sebastian. The cape itself, now part of the Oregon Parks and Recreation Department, was named by the Spanish navigator Sebastian Vizcaino in 1603 in honor of Saint Sebastian. (ODOT.)

A pull-off overlooking the ocean near Cape Sebastian offered travelers a view of the shoreline below. Such photographs were used by the highway department's Travel and Information Division to promote tourism. (ODOT.)

58

Brookings, with the nearby community of Harbor, served as the gateway to California. The town, located on the Chetco River, was dependent on supplies brought in by boat before the highway opened land access. Originally founded as a mill town, tourism quickly became an important industry for the area. (ODOT.)

The highway experienced immediate popularity with travelers, as evidenced by this line of automobiles marking the opening of a portion in Curry County. (Bandon HS.)

While the roadway continued into California, the section between Crescent City, California, and the connection with the Oregon Coast Highway was not a state highway. In 1922, the Oregon Highway Commission appealed to the state of California to designate that portion as part of their state highway system. The California legislature provided for the state to take over the existing county road in 1925, and the American Association of Highway Officials (AASHO) included that section in its designation of US Route 101 the following year. (ODOT.)

Five
Jeweled Clasps Along a Matched String of Pearls

By 1934, the entire route of the Oregon Coast Highway had been completed with at least an oiled finish. The exceptions were the waterways across Yaquina Bay at Newport, Alsea Bay at Waldport, the Siuslaw River at Florence, Coos Bay at Marshfield (now the City of Coos Bay), and the Umpqua River Bridge in Reedsport. (ODOT.)

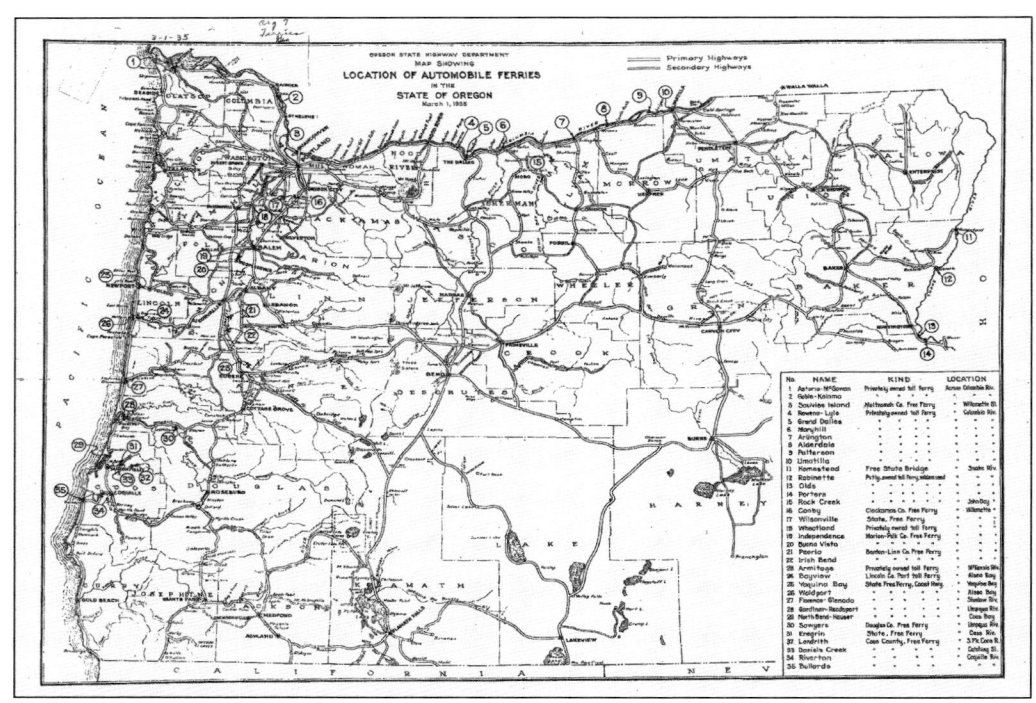

In anticipation of closing these gaps in the system and to encourage the expansion of tourism along the coast, the state took over private ferry services on these waterways. Intended to meet the needs of travelers while the bridges were being designed and constructed, these ferries offered free crossings for passenger vehicles. This 1935 map shows the location of automobile ferries in the state, including ones noted as "State Free Ferry, Coast Hwy." (ODOT.)

Conde McCullough had been teaching civil engineering at the Oregon Agricultural College— now Oregon State University—when the State Highway Department approached him in 1919 to come to Salem as the new state bridge engineer. McCullough accepted and quickly built a reputation of being able to combine functionality with aesthetics in his bridge designs. (ODOT.)

By the early 1930s, McCullough had already designed numerous bridges along the coast, including the one at Cape Creek (1932), part of the forest highway system near Heceta Head. It was reminiscent of ancient Roman aqueducts and the Depoe Bay Bridge (1927). (Both, ODOT.)

63

McCullough embraced the challenge of bridging the final gaps and set about designing and constructing the five major coastal bridges, depicted here in a representation by David Thompson. Drafting space at the headquarters building in Salem was limited, and design work was done in shifts. Ivan Merchant, a protege of McCullough's from Oregon Agricultural College who went on to serve as state bridge engineer from 1958 to 1972, recalled working on the designs: "I worked the night shift from 3 o'clock until midnight, and there was another crew in the morning because we had only so many desks. . . . Mac would lay out the overall job. . . . But Mac came in one day just after they had given me this job to work on [the main arch], and he just took a piece of paper and said, 'Now Ivan, this is about what you are going to do.' And he drew this spandrel arch in there and the roadway and, now there it is, go ahead." Federal Depression relief funds from the Public Works Administration were made available for building the bridges, and all five were designed and constructed between 1934 and 1936. Their magnificent spans and architectural features provided the perfect accent to the beautiful coastlines they spanned. McCullough himself referred to them as "jeweled clasps along a matched string of pearls." (ODOT.)

Work on a 160-foot and 180-foot arch in the construction of the Yaquina Bay Bridge is seen here in 1935 (ODOT.)

The completed span across Yaquina Bay in Newport was opened to the public on September 6, 1936, with a celebration on October 3. The arch bridge measured 3,260 feet in length. The distinctive green color of many of Oregon's bridges is attributed to McCullough's desire to avoid the stark black of earlier bridges. (ODOT.)

At Waldport, construction on the Alsea Bay Bridge is underway in this 1935 photograph. The bridge would measure 2,028 feet in length upon completion. (ODOT.)

The Alsea Bay Bridge was opened to the public on May 9, 1936. The bridge's construction required 20,000 cubic yards of concrete and 1,000 tons of reinforcing steel. (ODOT.)

Here, a crew works on the deck finish on the Siuslaw River Bridge in Florence. The 1,568-foot bridge cost $527,000 to build. (ODOT.)

The completed Siuslaw River Bridge shows the bascule and arch spans. The bridge opened with a ceremony on May 24, 1936. This bridge was the only one of the five to feature the bascule design, with a center span able to swing upward to accommodate river traffic. (ODOT.)

This 1935 photograph shows work being done on the Coos Bay Bridge. The cantilever bridge near North Bend was considered the longest bridge in Oregon at its completion, measuring 5,305 feet. It was also the most costly of the five bridges, with a $2.14 million price tag. (ODOT.)

A crew works on the north approach of the bridge. The construction crew employed 250 men working two shifts daily over a 30-hour work week. Common laborers earned 50¢ an hour, while semi-skilled workers earned 75¢. (ODOT.)

This is the view looking north from the east side of the completed Coos Bay Bridge. A three-day celebration was held for the dedication of this bridge on June 5–7, 1936. (ODOT.)

This was said to have been McCullough's personal favorite of the five bridges completed in 1936 and went on to bear his name, today known as both the Coos Bay Bridge and the McCullough Bridge. (ODOT.)

The arch and steel spans are taking shape in this photograph of the Umpqua River Bridge, a swing-span bridge located in Reedsport. The swing span design accommodated tall vessels common on the river. (ODOT.)

The Umpqua River Bridge was opened on July 2, 1936. It was the only one of this group of bridges that did not have a dedication ceremony. The completed bridge was 2,206 feet long and cost $510,500. (ODOT.)

Other McCullough designed coastal bridges include the Old Youngs Bay Bridge (1921) and the Lewis and Clark River Bridge (1924), both in the Astoria area, as well as the Rocky Creek Bridge near Otter Crest (1927), pictured here. This bridge is on a portion of the original highway that was later realigned. It is also known as the Ben F. Jones Memorial Bridge, after the author of the bill designating the Roosevelt Military Coast Highway. (ODOT.)

Another earlier bridge spanned the Rogue River between Gold Beach and Wedderburn, opening in 1932. (ODOT.)

By the mid-1980s, nearly 50 years after its construction, the damage to the Alsea Bay Bridge at Waldport from exposure to decades of the corrosive salt environment was considered to be irreversible by the highway department. The decision to replace the bridge was met with outcry and dismay at the thought of losing one of McCullough's iconic "pearls." However, by that time, the die was cast, and the cost to repair the bridge was prohibitive. An effort was made to mimic the original design when constructing the replacement, and the new span was built alongside the older bridge. (ODOT.)

The demolition of the original bridge began with a dramatic series of explosions in the fall of 1991. Fearing the loss of other historic coastal structures, Oregon pioneered a program of cathodic protection, which applied a low-voltage electric current to repel the effects of corrosion. This has ensured the public's continued enjoyment of Oregon's majestic bridges that span the waterways along the coast. (ODOT.)

Six
Pushing toward the Sea

While the Oregon Coast Highway was considered to have been completed when the five coastal bridges closed the last gaps to form a continuous roadway in 1936, much work remained to be done. Large portions of the highway had been hewn out of virgin forests, and rugged headlands led to steep grades and curves. As seen here, many stretches of the roadway were narrow, barely leaving room for two vehicles to pass. (ODOT.)

As standards were developed and construction techniques refined, the Coast Highway saw an evolution of improvement that continued throughout the years. This stretch between North Bend and Marshfield (now Coos Bay) shows a well-surfaced roadway and a standard lane width, but the lanes themselves are not delineated with striping. (ODOT.)

While several states vie for the title of being the first to implement centerline striping, Oregon is certainly one of the contenders, introducing the center stripe on portions of the Columbia River Highway in 1917. By the early 1930s, the department had begun to use a striping machine developed by OSHD employee and inventor O.E. Maynard. The lightweight striper, pushed in front of a truck, was able to stripe faster and more accurately than commercially available products of the time. This allowed Oregon construction crews to greatly increase the safety of the traveling public, and the design quickly became popular and used by other states. (ODOT.)

Maintaining what had been constructed was—and remains today—a constant struggle with the elements. Weather conditions often affected travel on the Coast Highway. Heavy winter rains and unstable, shifting ground along the coast gave way to flooding and landslides. This photograph shows flooding covering the roadway south of Coquille. (ODOT.)

A report in the 1953–1954 biennial report illustrated how destructive the winter storms could be to the roadway: "Western Oregon had a bad rain storm in January, 1953; 19 inches fell in five days at Gold Beach and slides and washouts were numerous along the Coast. There was considerable loss of cattle in Coos County, the logging industry was disrupted and several houses demolished. In Curry County over 200 slides blocked the Coast Highway." Flooding and landslides continue to affect the Coast Highway; in 1999, a major landslide north of Yachats blocked the highway completely for several months, forcing a lengthy detour. The earlier landslide pictured here closed a portion of the highway south of Glenada. (ODOT.)

During the years that the Coast Highway was being built, new standards and procedures were being implemented. The state was also committed to the idea of having the highway hug the coastline as closely as possible. Even before the highway was officially complete, plans were being made to realign some areas. (ODOT.)

In some cases, construction simply took out curves or widened the existing roadway; in others, an entirely new alignment was created. (ODOT.)

In this 1952 photograph of construction between Reedsport and Winchester Bay, the original roadway is visible and still in use while grading is taking place for the new alignment. (ODOT.)

In areas where no local roads were available for detours, long lines of traffic would sometimes form waiting for construction equipment to clear. (ODOT.)

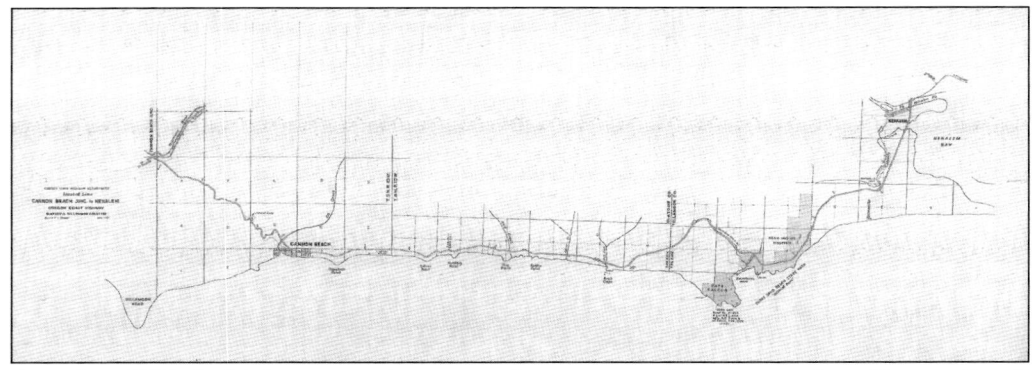

As early as 1932, the highway commission agreed to create an alternate route from Cannon Beach Junction—north of Cannon Beach where the Coast Highway intersected with Wolf Creek Highway (now the Sunset Highway)—to Nehalem. The original route in that area had turned inland and bypassed the popular resort town of Cannon Beach. Funding for construction was tight with the Depression-era economy, and the state had committed to the allotted number of miles within the state that could qualify for federal aid. The 1931–1932 biennial report stated that the previous US Congress had passed an emergency act permitting an extension of the system, giving Oregon an additional 418.1 miles available for federal-aid funding. The highway commission designated the route through Cannon Beach as part of this increased mileage. (ODOT.)

There was a good reason that the original highway had bypassed this area; the rugged terrain and the need for construction of several bridges and a tunnel created difficulties, and it would take nearly a decade to complete this section. This photograph shows construction work on the Hug Point to Arch Cape portion in 1933. (ODOT.)

The existing county road linking Cannon Beach with the Coast Highway was improved as the first part of this project. This aerial view of Cannon Beach shows the distinctive Haystack Rock off the coast. (ODOT.)

South of Cannon Beach, at Arch Cape, a decision was made to tunnel through the headland. The project began in 1936, but bad weather, equipment problems, and delays in obtaining the tunnel lining materials pushed the opening to March 1940. (ODOT.)

The resulting Arch Cape Tunnel was over 1,200 feet in length, 26 feet wide, and 23 feet high. This photograph shows the difficult conditions workers faced in the tunnel interior. (ODOT.)

The Necarney Creek Bridge was one of several bridges constructed during this project. Designed by state bridge engineer Glenn Paxson, it was completed in 1937. (ODOT.)

The Necarney Creek Bridge is also known as the Sam Reed Bridge, after the landowner who donated much of Neahkahnie Mountain to the state for the construction of the highway through that area. Reed and his wife built the Neahkahnie Inn in 1912. (Nehalem Valley HS.)

The name of the creek spanned by this bridge is almost certainly a variation of the name of nearby Neahkahnie Mountain. Spelling was somewhat more fluid in the days when the name was attached to the mountain, and even the origins of the name Neahkahnie have been disputed over the years. An early diary relates, "This mountain is called Ne-a-karny—after one of the deities of these natives, who, it is said by them, a long time since, while sitting on this mountain, turned into a stone, which stone, it is said, presents a colossal figure of Ne-a-karny to this day." Other explanations point to Neahkahnie being one of several Native American coastal villages—*Ne-* being the Clatsop Indian prefix for a place. One local story even points to the name originating with the survivors of a Spanish wreck off the coast exclaiming "carne"—the Spanish word for meat—on seeing elk on the mountain. Ironically, the bridge dedication plaque misidentifies it as the Neahkahnie Creek Bridge, an oversight that was never corrected. (ODOT.)

The Neahkahnie Mountain section offered its own challenges. Towering several hundred feet above the ocean, the grade was cut into the side of the mountain. This image of early work shows the difficult terrain. (ODOT.)

By the time this photograph was taken in 1940, the grade had been established. However, much work remained to stabilize the cliff sides. (ODOT.)

Crews worked on steep hillsides to prepare the rockwork along the roadway. This photograph was captioned, "Showing inclination of rock sloping towards future wall. This inclined plane is found beneath each layer." (ODOT.)

The bridge, parapet walls, and retaining walls along the Neahahnie Mountain section made use of native stone in their construction. (ODOT.)

Like the Necarny Creek Bridge, the Neahkahnie Chasm Bridge was also designed by bridge engineer Glenn Paxson. These photographs show it under construction and after completion. (Both, ODOT.)

The rockwork added additional interest to the magnificent vistas offered by the new route, as shown in these two images. (Both, ODOT.)

The new stretch of highway continued south of the Neahkahnie Mountain area toward the town of Manzanita. (ODOT.)

The town of Nehalem served as the southern endpoint for the new highway alignment. The original alignment served as the western end of the Wolf Creek (now Sunset) Highway, US Route 26, and then south from Necanicum as the Necanicum Highway, Oregon Route 53, to Nehalem Bay. (ODOT.)

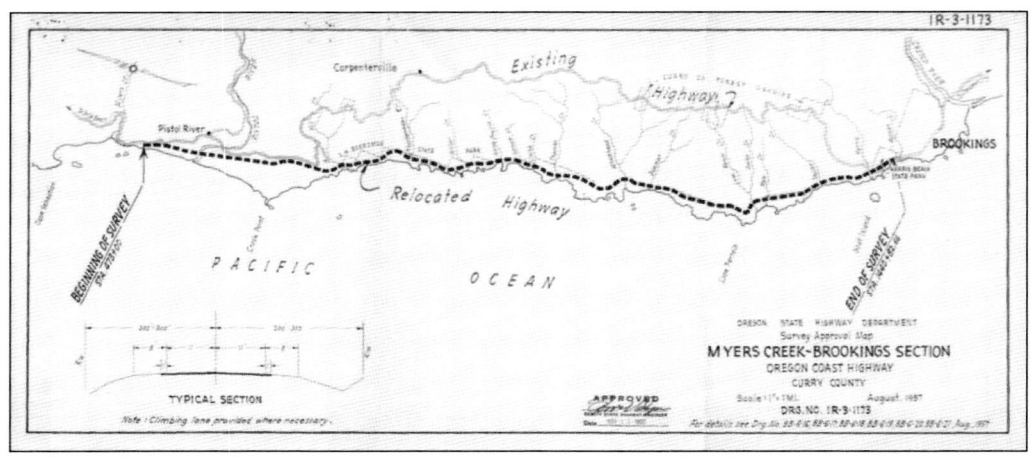

In the 1950s, two other major realignments again pushed the highway out to the coastline. In Curry County, the section from Pistol River to Brookings originally went inland from the coast. (ODOT.)

The realignment had the highway skirting headlands along the shoreline, such as shown here in a construction photograph in the area of Whale Head. (ODOT.)

The Thomas Creek Bridge was part of this project. At 340 feet in height, it remains the tallest bridge in Oregon. (ODOT.)

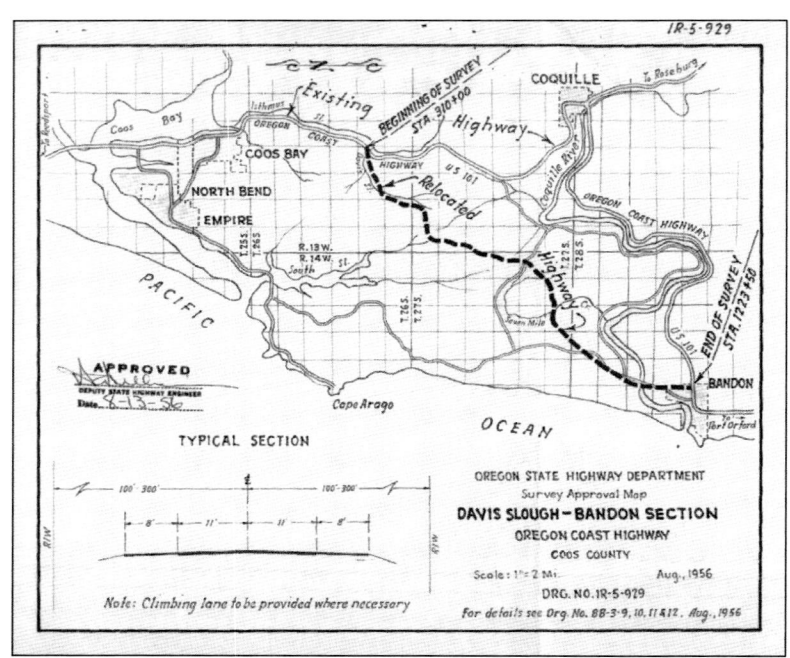

In Coos County, the former alignment passing through Coquille to Bandon was pushed westward to parallel the coastline. (ODOT.)

The earlier route remained on the state highway system. From the point where the realignment project began in the Davis Slough area to Coquille became part of Oregon Route 42. Oregon Route 42S carried the original alignment from Coquille to Bandon, rejoining the Coast Highway. (ODOT.)

Seven
OREGON STATE PARKS AND THE HIGHWAY DEPARTMENT

The history of the Oregon Parks and Recreation Department is intrinsically linked with the history of the Oregon Department of Transportation. From the time that Gov. Oswald West persuaded the state legislature to declare beaches along the entire state coast part of the state highway system, the groundwork was laid to develop points of interest and beauty for the enjoyment of the traveling public. Here, rocky terraces are seen on the coastline of Shore Acres State Park. (ODOT.)

The state recognized the value of tourism and the benefit that out-of-state travelers could bring to local economies. Camping had become a popular pastime, but few developed areas were available. In 1921, in response to an address by Gov. Ben Olcott, the Oregon legislature authorized the State Highway Commission to obtain lands outside of the highway right-of-way to establish and preserve areas of particular scenic beauty. This photograph shows a picnic area overlooking the ocean in Cape Arago State Park in Coos County. (ODOT.)

A letter from the state highway engineer dated September 1928 stated that nine park sites had already been acquired along the Coast Highway in Lincoln and Curry Counties, although no improvements had been made at that time. The northernmost of these early parks was Boiler Bay, named for the boiler of the steamer *J. Marhoffer*. (ODOT.)

In 1929, Samuel H. Boardman was appointed parks engineer. Boardman proved to be a capable administrator, and the parks program expanded greatly under his supervision. An outline of some of the early coastal parks and waysides follows. (ODOT.)

Improvements began in earnest in the early 1930s when the Civilian Conservation Corps (CCC) provided manpower to clear trails and construct buildings, camping, and picnic areas. This photograph shows picnic tables and an outdoor cooking area at Ecola State Park between Seaside and Cannon Beach. The park includes the promontory of Tillamook Head and derives its name from the Chinook Indian word for whale. (Parks.)

In addition to the potential for camping and picnicking, coastal parks were chosen for their dramatic views of the ocean, whether from the beach or from overlooks high above the surf. This is another view of Ecola showing the coastline as seen from the park. (ODOT.)

The highway at Neahkahnie Mountain south of Cannon Beach bisects Oswald West State Park, named for Gov. Oswald West, first chair of the Oregon Highway Commission. The park was originally called Short Sand Beach State Park; the name was changed in 1956. (ODOT.).

Cape Lookout, south of Tillamook, was renowned for its many species of birds. This state park lies west of the Coast Highway between Netarts Bay and the ocean. The initial land acquisition was a 1935 gift to the state from the US Lighthouse Service. (Parks.)

Surf pounds the coast below the Otter Crest Wayside, an area gifted to the state by Wilbur and Florence Badley in 1928. (ODOT.)

Adjoining the wayside, the Badleys later constructed their Look-Out coffee shop, which is now operated by the state as a gift shop. (ODOT.)

Highway department graphic artist Frank Hutchinson created this representation of proposed development for Otter Crest. Although the final development did not entirely follow this proposal, it shows the planning process that went into each part of the highway and parks construction. The Badleys' coffee/gift shop is shown to the back of the site. (ODOT.)

Just south of Otter Crest lies Devils Punchbowl State Park. Waves surge into the hollow rock formation—likely caused by the collapse of two sea cave roofs—and churn as if in a giant cauldron. (Parks.)

97

Beverly Beach State Park is seven miles north of Newport. This photograph looks to the north, toward Spencer Creek. The highway bridge over Spencer Creek allowed park visitors to pass under it to gain access to the beach area. (ODOT.)

The first land for Seal Rock Wayside south of Newport was obtained in 1929, with subsequent purchases bringing the total area to over four and a half acres. The park is named for the partially submerged chain of rocks off the shoreline known as Seal Rocks. Three of the larger rocks—named Castle Rock, Tourist Rock, and Elephant Rock—were obtained from the federal government in 1928. (Parks.)

Spouting horns, such as the one seen here at Cook's Chasm in Neptune State Park, are caused by wave action through water-carved tunnels that reach the surface near the shore. Spouting horns can be viewed in several locations, most famously off the downtown area in Depoe Bay. (ODOT.)

A calmer ocean is shown in this sunset photograph of driftwood and seagulls at Neptune State Park south of Yachats. This park is on both sides of the highway and now covers over 330 acres. (ODOT.)

Devil's Elbow State Park included a cove below Heceta Head Lighthouse. Established in 1930, the park was later part of an expansion that encompassed the lighthouse; today, the park is known as the Heceta Head Lighthouse Scenic Viewpoint, which also highlights the distinctive McCullough-designed Arch Cape Bridge. Heceta Head was named for Spanish navigator Bruno de Heceta, who explored the Oregon coast in 1775. (ODOT.)

The estate of Louis and Lela Simpson, known as Shore Acres, was purchased by the state in 1942. The mansion and formal gardens fell into some disrepair in the subsequent years, but beginning around 1970, work began to restore the grounds of Shore Acres State Park to their original beauty. The estate lies in the area of Cape Arago, and the park adjoins Cape Arago State Park. (Parks.)

Humbug Mountain State Park spans both sides of the highway south of Port Orford. Named for the 1,742-foot Humbug Mountain, the park boasts almost four miles of coastline. Acquisition of land for this park began in 1926. (Bandon HS.)

In this early photograph, the highway cuts through Cape Sebastian State Park south of the town of Gold Beach in Curry County. Land for the park was first acquired in 1925, and it bears the name of the promontory it occupies. (ODOT.)

Cape Sebastian State Park offered dramatic views of the coast and beach area. Today, the park totals more than 1,400 acres and is known as the Cape Sebastian Scenic Corridor. (Parks.)

Harris Beach State Park lies just north of the city of Bandon in Curry County. It offers views of an offshore rookery that still boasts breeding grounds for birds, including the tufted puffin. The park was named for George Harris, an early resident of the Bandon area who owned the land that makes up the park. (Parks.)

Eight
LIGHTHOUSES OF THE OREGON COAST

For the most part, the coastal lighthouses predated the Oregon Coast Highway, but many have been absorbed into the Oregon Parks and Recreation system over the years. At the time the highway was being built, all the lighthouses were functional, with the exception of the Yaquina Bay Lighthouse, which had been replaced by the brighter and better situated Yaquina Head Lighthouse. The lighthouses, active or not, have remained a point of interest for visitors traveling the highway. This photograph shows the Cape Meres Lighthouse with its short 38-foot tower. (ODOT.)

Nicknamed "Terrible Tilly" because of its exposure to severe storm waves, the Tillamook Rock Lighthouse was built on a basalt rock islet to guide ships entering the Columbia River. It was first lit in 1881 and was replaced by a whistle buoy in 1957. Now privately owned, the lighthouse at one time operated as a columbarium for the storage of funeral urns. (ODOT.)

Cape Meares Lighthouse perches atop a narrow spit of land jutting out into the ocean. This lighthouse is now managed by the Oregon Parks and Recreation Department and is part of the Cape Meares State Scenic Viewpoint west of Tillamook. (Parks.)

The Yaquina Head Lighthouse north of Newport has a 93-foot tower, the tallest on the coast. It continues to guide ships and today is managed by the federal Bureau of Land Management. (ODOT.)

The Yaquina Bay Lighthouse only operated for three years, from 1871 to 1874, after which it was replaced by the taller and brighter Yaquina Head Lighthouse. Today, this is the only wood lighthouse in Oregon, and the only existing example in the state of the tower being combined with the keeper's residence. The building fell into disrepair and was slated for destruction, but community support led to the restoration of the building and grounds. The lamp was relit in 1996 as a privately maintained aid to navigation. The lighthouse is part of Yaquina Bay State Park. (Oregon Historical Society.)

Heceta Head Lighthouse north of Florence rises 205 feet above the ocean. Now part of the Heceta Head State Scenic Viewpoint, the light was first lit in 1894 and continues to operate with an automated beacon that reaches 21 miles out into the ocean. (ODOT.)

The Cape Creek Bridge, designed by Conde McCullough, can easily be seen just to the south of the Heceta Head lighthouse complex. (ODOT.)

The first lighthouse built at the site of the present Umpqua River Lighthouse fell victim to shore erosion in 1861, just four years after it was constructed. The current structure was first illuminated in 1894 and continues to operate. It is part of Umpqua Lighthouse State Park near Reedsport. (ODOT.)

Starting operations in 1934, the Cape Arago Lighthouse is the third lighthouse to occupy an islet near Cape Arago. The islet was originally connected to the mainland by a bridge, which has since been taken down, and the lighthouse is not open to the public. It can be seen in the background of this photograph from Sunset Bay State Park. (ODOT.)

Located in Bullards Beach State Park near Bandon, the Coquille River Lighthouse originally guided boats across a dangerous bar. Operating from 1896, the lighthouse was decommissioned in 1939 following improvements to the river channel. (Parks.)

Cape Blanco Lighthouse near Port Orford is the oldest standing lighthouse on the Oregon coast. Built in 1870, the lighthouse served to warn ships of the reefs extending from the cape; the shipping in the area primarily supported the lumber and mining industries. It is now part of Cape Blanco State Park and operates with automated lights. (Parks.)

Nine
Impact of the Oregon Coast Highway

The construction of the Oregon Coast Highway changed the lives of the state's coastal residents, boosting the economies of the coastal communities at a time when many areas were seeing a downturn in local industries. This photograph shows a street scene in Newport in the 1940s. (Lincoln Co. HS.)

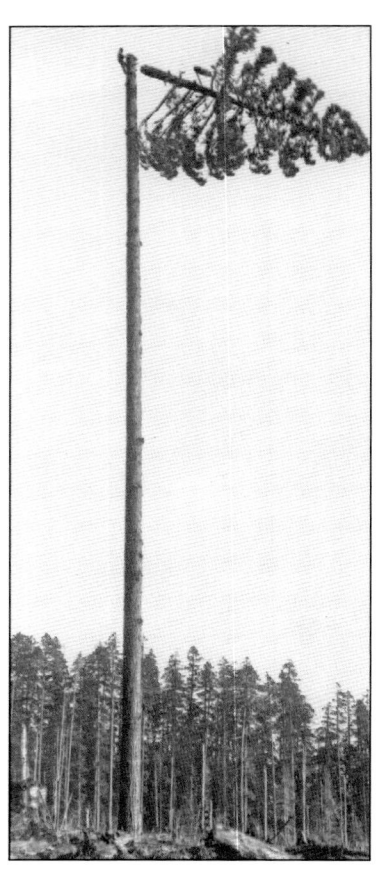

The United States' involvement in World War I had brought considerable growth to the coast's logging, milling, and shipbuilding businesses. With the end of the war and the cancellation of government orders, the industry declined. Although rebounding somewhat by the late 1920s, coastal logging never regained wartime production levels. This image shows the process of topping a 200-foot spar tree—the tree used as the highest anchor point in a cable logging setup—in Clatsop County. (ODOT.)

Despite the economic downturn, many communities continued to rely on traditional natural resource–based industries, including commercial fishing and logging. Boats are seen here leaving the harbor at Depoe Bay, a town well known for its commercial and charter fleets. (ODOT.)

This glass slide photograph shows the huge salmon yield gathered as the fish entered the coastal rivers to return to their breeding grounds. (ODOT.)

The construction of the highway brought changes in the way established industries operated. While logging operations had traditionally relied on railroads to transport the logs from the forest to the mills, logging trucks now became the norm on the roadways. Graphic artist Frank Hutchinson created drawings illustrating how signage should be used to alert drivers in areas where these large trucks would be entering the roadway. (ODOT.)

While traditional industries were finding new ways of doing business and transporting goods, a significant number of businesses saw the access provided by the highway as an incentive to shift their focus toward meeting the needs of the ever-growing tourist trade. Many communities had well-established reputations as vacation destinations before the highway was built, but they tended to cater primarily to the well-off who could afford the train or steamer rides to reach coastal resort towns and to rent rooms or even lease a home for the summer season. Suddenly, automobiles were being mass-produced and becoming affordable for working-class families. Moderately-priced cabins and motels began to spring up. This photograph shows the popular White's Cabins in Oceanlake. (Lincoln Co. HS.)

A 1939 travel brochure touted the state's reasonable prices for tourist facilities: "This is not a state of artificialities, of resorts designed only for the wealthy, of hotels and stopping places catering only to one of larger means. Rooms with bath can be obtained in first-class hotels from $2.00 to $4.00. Perfectly satisfactory accommodations may be had for less. Good auto camp cabins may be obtained from $1.00 to around $3.00 a night. One may rent boats for fishing for from $1.00 to $2.00 a day." Camping was becoming a popular form of sight-seeing, increasing pressure for the state to establish camping facilities in the state parks; here, a camper in Curry County is seen feeding a motherless fawn in the 1920s. (ODOT.)

The Travel and Information Division was formed as part of the Oregon Highway Department in 1935, and this group immediately launched a nationwide campaign to promote tourism in the state. In 1936—the year that the Coast Highway was completed—the department spent approximately $48,000 in its advertising and publicity program "setting forth the scenic and recreational attractions of Oregon accessible to the motoring world through the state's modern highway system," according to the 1935–1936 biennial report. Even the state highway map featured a sketch of the Oregon coastline. (ODOT.)

113

The scenic photographs used in advertisements distributed to popular journals and magazines lured many to visit the state, and a good percentage of these tourists came to see the newly completed Coast Highway. The year following the completion of the coastal bridges saw a remarkable 72 percent increase in visitors to the coast; attendance at the state parks along the coast grew at a rate of 20 percent or more per year between 1938 and 1940. Sites such as Sea Lion Caves, which were mostly inaccessible prior to the highway's construction, became thriving enterprises. (Sea Lion Caves.)

The advent of World War II and the Japanese bombing of Pearl Harbor brought significant changes to the tourist trade along the coast, as well as to the operations of the Oregon Highway Department in general. Gas rationing and travel restrictions limited visitors. The Travel and Information Division stopped actively promoting tourism, instead doing limited newspaper and magazine advertising to keep "the name 'Oregon' in the minds of prospective future travelers," according to the 1943–1944 biennial report. The publicity carried the message to "buy war bonds and stamps now and visit Oregon after the war is won." The same report showed the impact of tourism across the state up to that time, stating, "During the interval between 1935 and Pearl Harbor, tourist travel in Oregon increased over 50 per cent, becoming the third largest business in the state from the standpoint of income." (ODOT.)

Concerns over a coastal invasion led to heightened military patrols and new regulations for citizens. Where the highway ran along the coastline, drivers were required to provide shielding for their headlights after dark. (ODOT.)

115

Popular tourist attractions were taken over as military observation posts, including the estate of Shore Acres State Park at Cape Arago, and the Look-Out gift and coffee shop near Otter Crest. Troops stationed at these outposts monitored the shoreline for signs of Japanese submarines. Blimp patrols, stationed at the naval air base at Tillamook, were used to scan the coastline. Here, a blimp is seen behind the Look-Out post. (Parks.)

With the loss of manpower to the military and wartime industries and the scarcity of materials due to the war effort, much of the scheduled road construction work was postponed during this period. Women were hired to fill in on maintenance crews, as in this example of a female roller operator. (ODOT.)

Fort Stevens in Clatsop County was manned with troops from the 249th Coast Artillery of the Oregon National Guard and the 18th Coast Artillery of the US Army. This 1943 photograph shows wartime activity at the fort. The concerns over Japanese activity off the coast were not without merit—several submarine sightings were reported. Local history tells of a caretaker at Cape Sebastian State Park checking the trail to the cape around 1942 and hearing voices along the shore. The fog lifted and revealed a Japanese submarine surfaced to recharge its batteries. The caretaker apparently retreated to inform the Coast Guard, but a subsequent search found no sign of the submarine. In another incident, Fort Stevens itself was fired upon. On June 21, 1942, a submarine launched 17 shells toward Fort Stevens, none of them actually hitting it. In fact, the only casualty of the attack was a soldier who cut his head while rushing to man his battle station. In September 1942, a Japanese plane dropped an incendiary, or firebomb, in a forested area near Brookings, with the intention of creating a forest fire. The resulting fires were relatively small and quickly spotted, and were contained by a local forest service lookout. (Parks.)

With the end of World War II, the state once again launched a widespread campaign promoting tourism, claiming, "You'll Remember Oregon!" Scenic views of the coast were prominently featured in the promotional materials, and the flow of visitors to the area continued to increase. Tourism remains one of the top industries of the coast, along with fishing and logging. (ODOT.)

Ten
THE FINAL CHAPTER

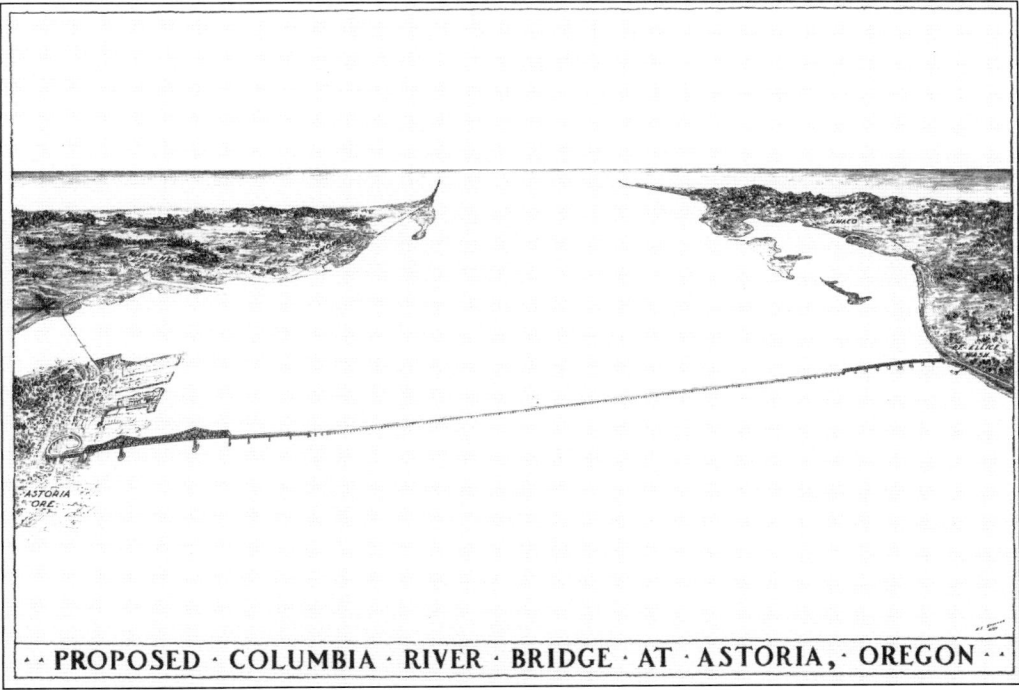

·· PROPOSED · COLUMBIA · RIVER · BRIDGE · AT · ASTORIA , · OREGON ··

US Route 101 was intended to extend from the Canadian to the Mexican borders, including the span across the Columbia River between Astoria, Oregon, and Megler, Washington. Plans for a bridge across this expanse began to gain momentum by the mid-1950s. Graphic artist Harold Spooner drew this representation of the proposed structure. (ODOT.)

For many years, this crossing was serviced by ferries, which began as early as 1840 with canoes. In 1921, Capt. Fritz Elfving established a commercial ferry business. The *Tourist No. 2*, pictured here, started service in 1924 and had a capacity of 20 cars and 155 passengers. During World War II, it was commandeered by the Army to lay mines in the lower river and act as a military ferry between Fort Canby on the Long Beach Peninsula in Washington and Fort Stevens in Oregon. After the war, it was sold back to Elfving's Astoria–North Beach Ferry Company. (ODOT.)

In 1946, the State Highway Department purchased three ferries from the Astoria–North Beach Ferry Company, including *Tourist No. 2*, *Tourist No. 3*, and the *North Beach*. However, the *North Beach* proved to be in poor condition and was scrapped in 1948. In the winter months, the ferries made 10 trips per day; in summer this increased to 20 trips per day, but demand continued to increase. In an attempt to meet this demand, the state contracted with the Albina Engine and Machine Works in Portland to build a new ferry for the Astoria-Megler route. (ODOT.)

The ferry was named the *M.R. Chessman* in tribute to state highway commissioner Merle R. Chessman. The 172-foot vessel was able to transport 44 vehicles and 416 passengers. It cost $500,000 and was launched in December 1947. (ODOT.)

Ferry service on the four-and-a-half-mile route was a half-hour trip in good weather, and despite the addition of the *Chessman*, long waits would occur during the summer tourist season. Additionally, the ferry service proved to be expensive, causing a loss of $2 million for the highway department from 1947 through the construction of the bridge in 1966. The unpredictable weather in the area also affected the ferry service. A newspaper article from November 1950 related that the *Chessman* had been lost for four hours in the fog after going off course. (ODOT.)

·· ASTORIA · BRIDGE · MAIN · CHANNEL · CROSSING ··

In 1954, Oregon and Washington entered into an agreement to conduct a preliminary survey, estimate of cost and traffic, and financial feasibility for the construction of a bridge over the Columbia River. In 1957, both states enacted legislation authorizing further engineering studies. By 1961, both states agreed to the project, funded by bonds that would be recouped through tolls. (ODOT.)

Ground-breaking ceremonies took place on August 9, 1962, with Gov. Mark Hatfield turning the first shovel of dirt. Actual construction began on November 5, 1962. (ODOT.)

The final length of the steel cantilever through-truss bridge was over four miles, and it remains the longest continuous truss bridge in North America. (ODOT.)

Truss construction was beginning in this 1964 photograph. A barge-mounted tower with a crane is helping to place the steel. (ODOT.)

The bridge was completed in 1966. It included 48,500 cubic yards of structural excavation, 158,785 linear feet of steel piling, 134 linear feet of timber piling, 76,496 linear feet of 14-inch pre-stressed concrete piling, 38,772 linear feet of 48-inch round pre-stressed concrete piling, 97,995 cubic yards of concrete, 6,005 tons of metal reinforcing, 15,500 tons of structural steel, 43,290 linear feet of aluminum parapet rail, and 440,000 board feet of treated lumber. Seven 354-foot-long steel through-truss spans cross the channel on the Washington side. The jetties at the mouth of the Columbia River can be seen in the background of this photograph. (ODOT.)

The ferry *Chessman* is pictured on one of its final runs as the bridge was being completed, signaling the end of an era. (ODOT.)

The toll facilities were located on the Oregon side, and travelers going in both directions paid a toll on this end. (ODOT.)

The bridge was opened to the public with a four-day celebration beginning on August 27, 1966, with a speech by Gov. Mark Hatfield. A parade through Astoria included the Astoria Clown Cars. This group had promoted the bridge by painting the slogan, "Let's build the bridge," on the 1948 Chrysler they used in parades. The celebration also included a salmon derby and sailboat races. The opening of the bridge closed the last gap for uninterrupted travel on US Route 101. (ODOT.)

The bonds for the bridge were paid off in late 1993, marking the end of the tolls. The celebration of the removal of the toll was held on December 24, 1993. An Astoria Clown Car was the first vehicle to pass through without a toll. (ODOT.)

Bibliography

Armstrong, Chester. *History of the Oregon State Parks.* Salem, OR: Oregon State Highway Department, 1965.

Beckham, Dow. *Bandon By-The-Sea: Hope and Perseverance in a Southwestern Oregon Town.* Bandon, OR: Bandon Historical Society, 1986.

Bottenberg, Ray. *Bridges of the Oregon Coast.* Charleston, SC: Arcadia Publishing, 2006.

"Coos History Museum." *Timeline of South Coast History.* Accessed November 4, 2018. https://cooshistory.org/research/timeline-of-south-coast-history/.

Crossley, Rod, and Margaret L. Rice. *Soldiers in the Woods: The U.S. Army's Spruce Production Division in World War One.* Portland, OR: TimberTimes Inc., 2014.

"Diary of Joseph H. Frost." *Oregon Historical Quarterly* 35 (n.d.).

Gaines, William. "Coast Artillery Organizational History, 1917–1950 Part I, Coast Artillery Regiments 1-196." The *Coast Defense Journal* 23, no. 2 (2009): 4–51.

Gordon, Greg. "Astoria and Columbia River Railroad." *The Oregon Encyclopedia: A Project of the Oregon Historical Society,* n.d.

Hadlow, Robert W. *Elegant Arches, Soaring Spans: C.B. McCullough, Oregon's Master Bridge Builder.* Corvallis, OR: Oregon State University Press, 2001.

McArthur, Lewis. *Oregon Geographic Names.* Oregon Historical Society Press, n.d.

Meier, Gary. "When the Highway Was Sand." *Oregon Coast,* February 1991.

Merchant, Ivan. Interview by Louis Pierce regarding Ivan Merchant's recollection of working on the Oregon Coastal bridges with Conde McCullough, June 4, 1980.

Oregon State Highway Commission. *Biennial Report of the Oregon State Highway Commission,* various years.

Oregon State University Special Collections and Archives. "Spruce Production Division: Were They Soldiers or Loggers? Were They Both?" n.d. www.flickr.com/photos/osucommons/sets/72157614450103966/.

Saubert, Steve, Kayleigh Anderson, and Carol Taylor. *Sea Lion Caves.* Greatland Classic Sales Co., n.d.

Schroeder, Walt. *They Found Gold on the Beach: A History of Central Curry County.* Curry County Historical Society Press, 1999.

Discover Thousands of Local History Books
Featuring Millions of Vintage Images

Arcadia Publishing, the leading local history publisher in the United States, is committed to making history accessible and meaningful through publishing books that celebrate and preserve the heritage of America's people and places.

Find more books like this at
www.arcadiapublishing.com

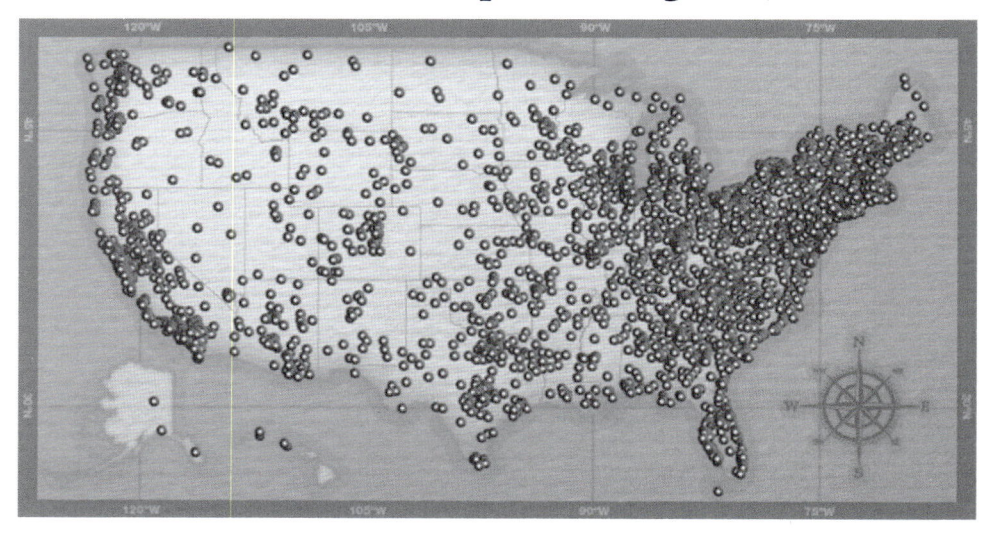

Search for your hometown history, your old stomping grounds, and even your favorite sports team.

Consistent with our mission to preserve history on a local level, this book was printed in South Carolina on American-made paper and manufactured entirely in the United States. Products carrying the accredited Forest Stewardship Council (FSC) label are printed on 100 percent FSC-certified paper.

MADE IN THE USA